# Enrichment Units in Math

Written by Judy Leimbach

Illustrated by Elisa Ahlin

## Attribute Blocks

## Tangrams

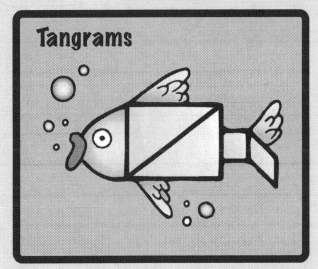

## Sets and Venn Diagrams

## Ancient Egyptian Numbers

# Contents

First published in 2009 by Prufrock Press Inc.

Published in 2021 by Routledge
605 Third Avenue, New York, NY 10017
2 Park Square, Milton Park, Abingdon, Oxon OX14 4RN

*Routledge is an imprint of the Taylor & Francis Group, an informa business.*

ISBN-13: 978-1-5936-3068-3  (pbk)

DOI: 10.4324/9781003235019

# Information for the Instructor

Mathematics is more than simply performing computations or memorizing basic facts. It is present all around us, from the designs in granny's quilt to the patterns on our floors and walls. Mathematics is concerned with making sense of the world around us. Mathematical thinking helps us make connections, to see order and logic.

Our students should be provided with a variety of opportunities to explore mathematical ideas in ways that promote their intellectual growth and expand their views of what mathematics is. This book provides four enrichment units that involve students actively and intellectually in mathematical thinking.

## 1. Challenging Attribute Block Activities

Students will sharpen thinking skills as they sort attribute logic blocks by similar attributes and by differences. The difference puzzles challenge students to reason logically and help them develop persistence in solving problems. It is an essential part of the learning process for students to realize they will not always be able to come up with a quick, right answer. Many of our brightest students will not develop perseverance unless we provide them with challenging activities that require them to persevere.

## 2. Set Analysis and Venn Diagrams

Reasoning and logical thinking are important components of mathematics. As stated in *Curriculum and Evaluation Standards for School Mathematics* issued by the National Council of Teachers of Mathematics (1989), ". . . critical thinking should be at the heart of instruction." The activities in this unit provide opportunities for critical thinking as students analyze attributes, form theories, test their theories, draw logical conclusions, and justify their answers. Bright students will enjoy the intellectual challenge!

## 3. Tangram Puzzles

The NCTM standards state that "Spatial understandings are necessary for interpreting, understanding, and appreciating our inherently geometric world . . .To develop spatial sense, children must have many experiences that focus on geometric relationships: the directions, orientation, and perspectives of objects . . ." Tangram activities actively involve students in solving puzzles that sharpen intuitions and awareness of spatial concepts. Comparing shapes in various positions will help develop their spatial sense. Students' spatial capabilities may differ from their numerical skills; therefore, tangram puzzles can be an excellent enrichment option for students who have mastered the numerical skills others in the class may still be working on. These activities can help develop persistence in students who usually find math easy but whose spatial capabilities may not be as advanced as their numerical skills.

## 4. Egyptian Number System

Studying other number systems helps students see mathematics as a language. It furthers their understanding of the symbolism of mathematics. It enriches their "number sense" and their appreciation of place value in our decimal system, a critical step in the development of number concepts. This unit would be an excellent enrichment option for students who have demonstrated their understanding of place value.

## How to Use the Units

The materials in this book may be used as extension units for the whole class or as enrichment for individuals or small groups.

While all students should have opportunities to explore mathematical ideas and to go beyond practicing computational skills, for the able math student who has demonstrated mastery of concepts being taught in the classroom, enrichment options are a necessity. These units are designed to help the classroom teacher provide for these needs. They lend themselves easily to a math center arrangement with each student having an individual folder and a checklist to record progress. Some of the units, such as the pattern block and tangram activities, can be ongoing throughout the year with students working on them whenever they are excused from other assignments or other work is completed.

Providing enrichment options need not be burdensome to the teacher. While the teacher may want to check some of the work himself/herself, it is not necessary for everything to be checked by the teacher as it is completed. Work can be checked by another student or self-corrected. Tangram puzzles, for example, can be checked by any other student with just a quick look. Answer keys can be provided

DOI: 10.4324/9781003235019-1

for checking other units (except for attribute blocks where answers will vary).

Remember, the emphasis for enrichment units is not "How many right?" or "How quickly did you finish?" The emphasis should be on promoting thinking, developing perseverance, expanding students' view of mathematics, enjoying a challenge, and on keeping able math students actively involved and enthusiastic about math.

# Materials

The following is a list of materials that your students will need for each of the four units in this book.

## Attribute Blocks

- a set of pocket-size attribute blocks
- pencil
- crayons or colored pencils

## Sets and Venn Diagrams

- pencil

## Tangrams

- set of tangrams (recommended)
  or
- scissors to cut out tangram set that is given
- Note: If you use certain commercial sets of tangrams, the shapes may not be exactly the same size as those shown in this book. It is possible to rnake the general configuration with any set of tangrams, but the size of the shapes may be slightly different than what is shown in this book.

## Ancient Egyptian Numbers

- pencil

Name _____

I began this unit on attribute blocks on _____.

Mark off each activity after you have completed it and after it has been checked. Hand in all pages when you finish the unit.

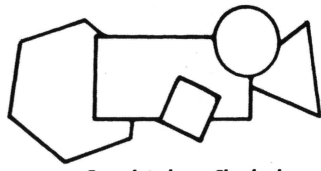

| *Lesson* | *Completed* | *Checked* |
|---|---|---|
| 1. Introduction | _____ | _____ |
| 2. Sorting by Attributes | _____ | _____ |
| 3. Sorting by Differences | _____ | _____ |
| 4. Sorting by One Difference | _____ | _____ |
| 5. Sorting by One and Two Differences | _____ | _____ |
| 6. Make a One-Difference Chain | _____ | _____ |
| 7. Make a Two-Difference Chain | _____ | _____ |
| 8. Make a Three-Difference Chain | _____ | _____ |
| 9. Make a Two-Difference Connecting Chain | _____ | _____ |
| 10. Make a Connecting Chain | _____ | _____ |
| 11. Difference Puzzle A | _____ | _____ |
| 12. Difference Puzzle B | _____ | _____ |
| 13. Difference Puzzle C | _____ | _____ |
| 14. Difference Puzzle D | _____ | _____ |
| 15. Difference Puzzle E | _____ | _____ |

I completed this unit on _____

Name _____

Attribute blocks differ from each other in four ways. They are different:

    ***Shape*** - circles, squares, rectangles, triangles, and hexagons

    ***Color*** - red, yellow, and blue

    ***Size*** - big and little

    ***Thickness*** - thin and thick

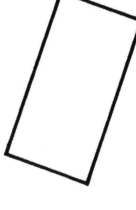
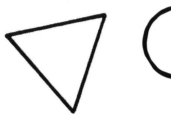

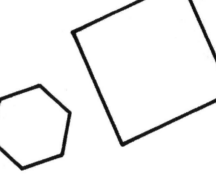
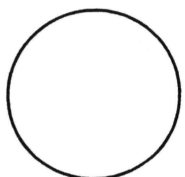

Choose a **little, blue, thick** shape to put in the circle. Trace around the shape. Color it blue. Mark it with **TH** for thick.

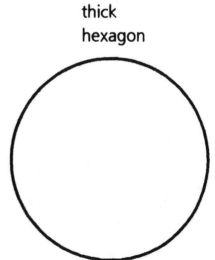

Place the correct attribute block in each circle below. Trace around each shape. Color it and mark **th** for thin or **TH** for thick.

| small | big | big |
| --- | --- | --- |
| blue | red | yellow |
| thick | thin | thick |
| triangle | square | hexagon |

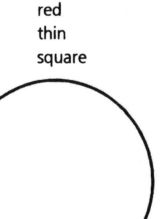

Name _____

Study the diagram at the right. Then use the diagram below to sort blocks into sets. Place **two** blocks in each square. Trace and color the shapes.

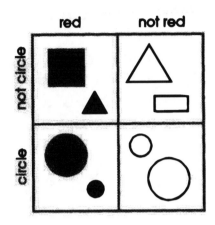

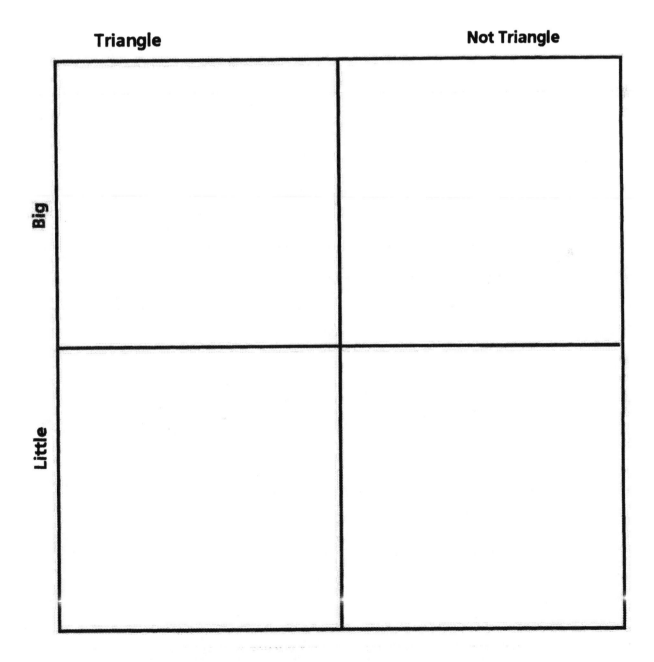

Name _____

Choose any attribute block and place it in the circle. After you have placed the blocks on this page, trace around the shapes, color them, and mark them **th** for thin or **TH** for thick.

1. In this row, place 3 blocks that differ in just **one way** from the block in the circle.

2. In this row, place 3 blocks that differ in **two ways** from the block in the circle.

3. In this row, place 3 blocks that differ in **three ways** from the block in the circle.

Name ____________________

Put blocks in the empty spaces in the grid so that the blocks in each row have **one** different attribute and the blocks in each column have **one** different attribute. Trace around the blocks and color them. Write **th** for thin and **TH** for thick.

**One Difference**

**One Difference**

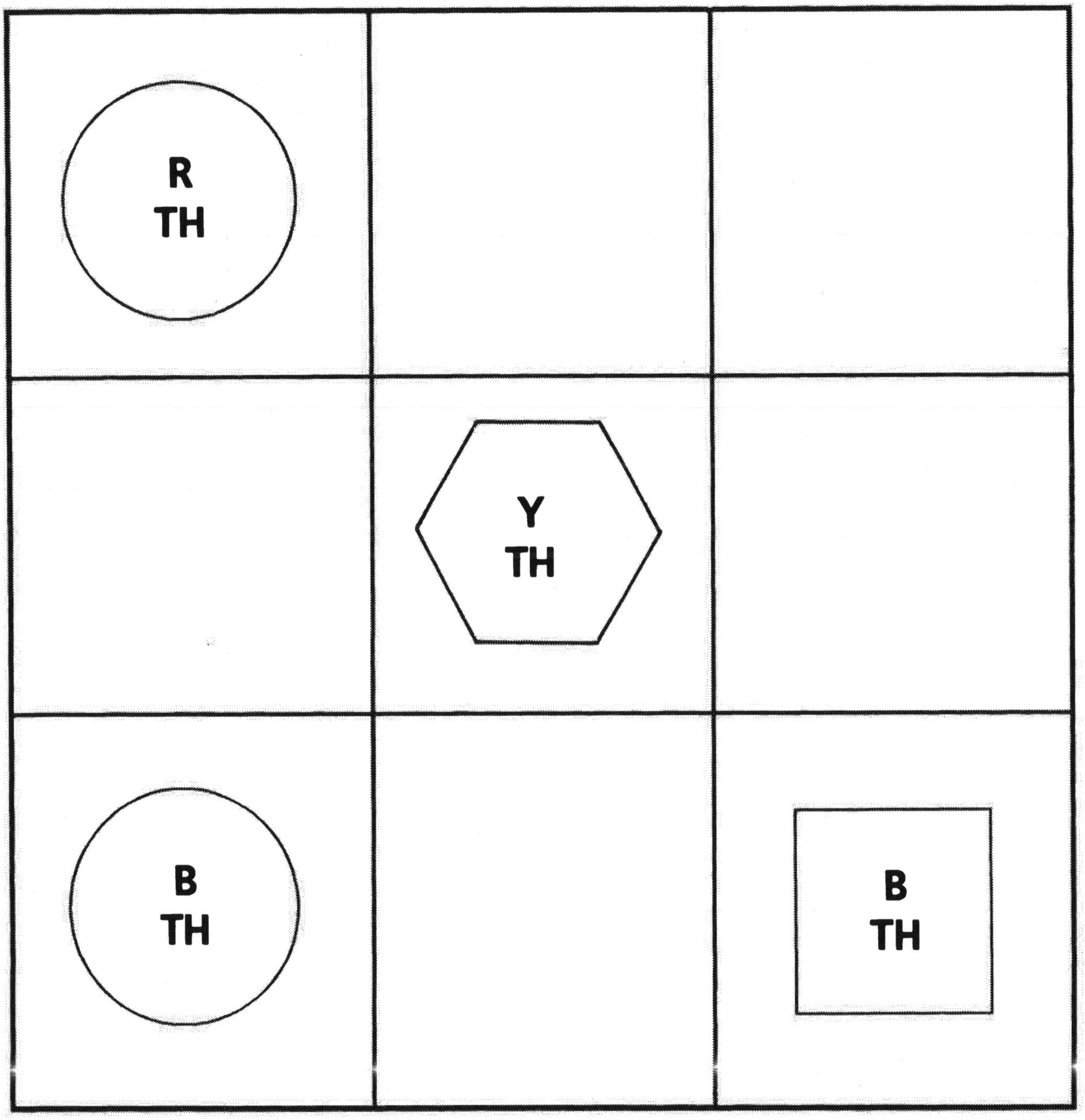
R
TH
Y
TH
B
TH
B
TH

Name _____

Put blocks in the empty spaces in the grid so that the blocks in each row have **one** different attribute and the blocks in each column have **two** different attributes. Trace around the blocks and color them. Write **th** for thin and **TH** for thick.

**One Difference**

| | | |
|---|---|---|
| | B<br>TH | |
| Y<br>th | | R<br>th |
| Y<br>TH | | |

*Two Differences*

Name _____

Place a **big, blue, thin rectangle** in the first link of the chain. Put blocks in the other circles so each block is different in **one way** (size, color, thickness or shape) from the blocks next to it. Trace and color the shapes. Mark each shape **th** for thin or **TH** for thick.

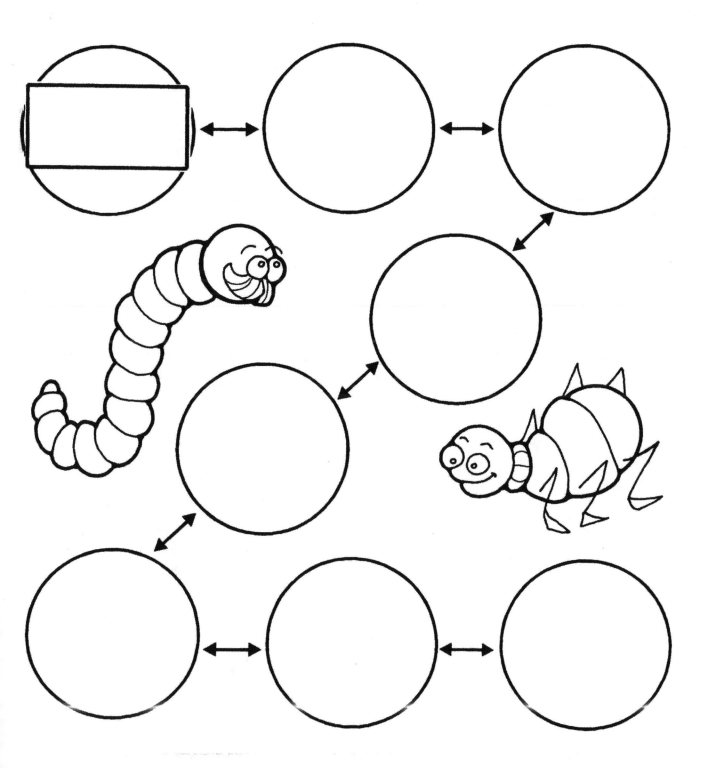

Name _____

Place a **small, red, thick circle** in the first link of the chain. Put blocks in the other circles so each block is different in **two ways** (size, color, thickness or shape) from the blocks next to it. Trace and color the shapes. Mark each shape **th** for thin or **TH** for thick.

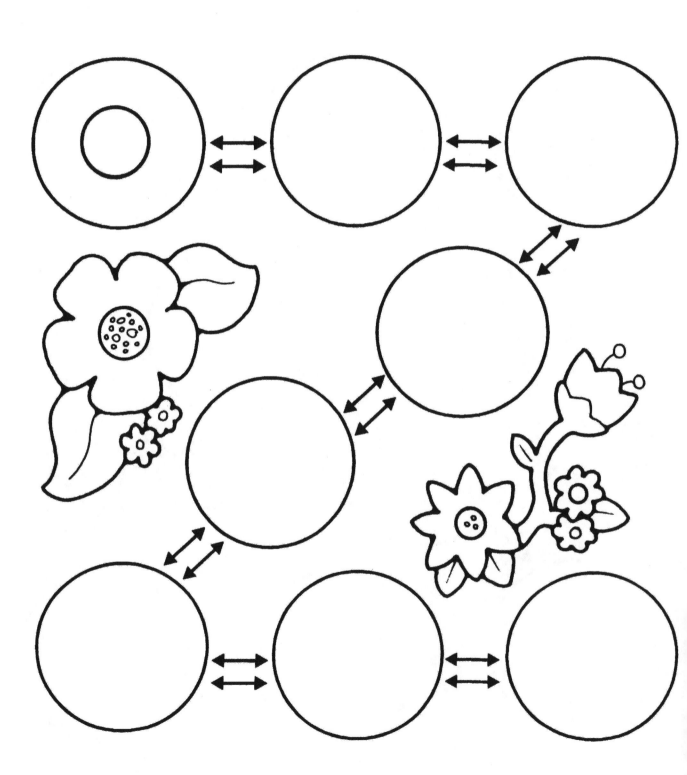

Name _____

Place a **big, yellow shape** in the first link of the chain. Put blocks in the other circles so each block is different in **three ways** (size, color, thickness or shape) from the blocks next to it. Trace and color the shapes. Mark each shape **th** for thin or **TH** for thick.

Name _____

Make a connecting difference chain by putting blocks in the circles so that each link will have **two differences** from the links on each side of it. Trace and color the shapes. Mark each shape **th** for thin or **TH** for thick.

Name _____

The number of arrows will tell you how many differences there should be between the blocks in the chain. Trace and color the shapes. Mark each shape **th** for thin or **TH** for thick.

Name _____

The number of arrows will tell you how many differences there should be between the blocks in each circle. Trace and color the shapes. Mark each one **th** for thin or **TH** for thick.

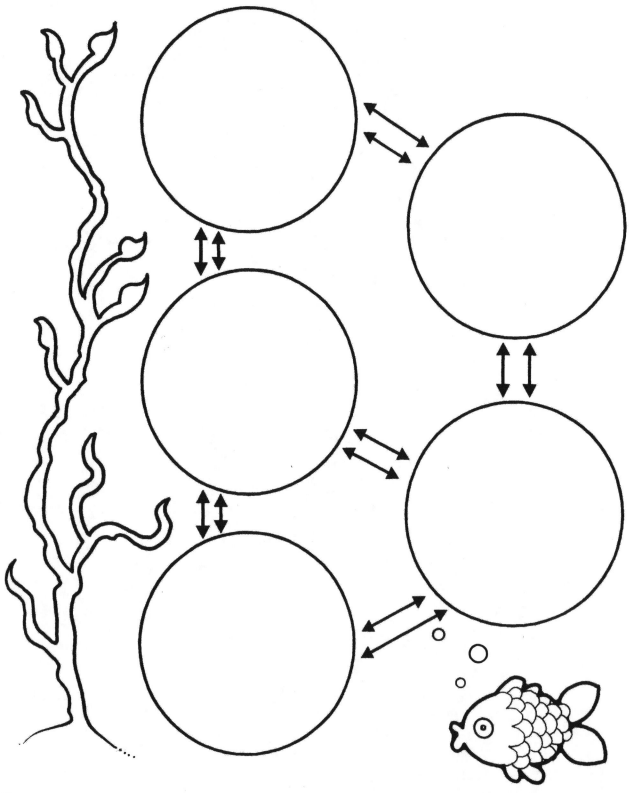

Name _____

The number of arrows will tell you how many differences there should be between the blocks in each circle. Trace and color the shapes. Mark each one **th** for thin or **TH** for thick.

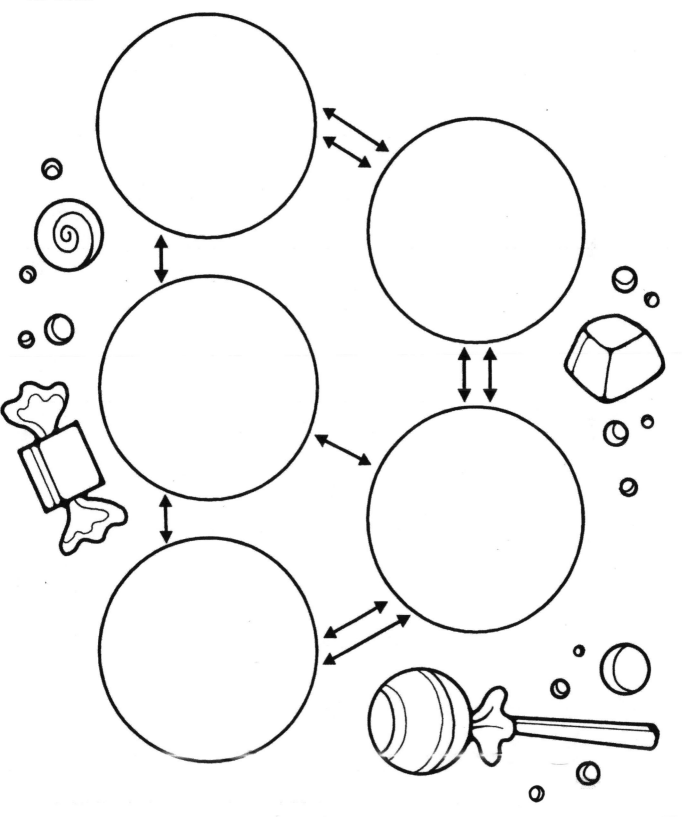

Name _____

The number of arrows will tell you how many differences there should be between the blocks in each circle. Trace and color the shapes. Mark each one **th** for thin or **TH** for thick.

Name _____

The number of arrows will tell you how many differences there should be between the blocks in each circle. Trace and color the shapes. Mark each one **th** for thin or **TH** for thick.

Name _____

The number of arrows will tell you how many differences there should be between the blocks in each circle. Trace and color the shapes. Mark each one **th** for thin or **TH** for thick.

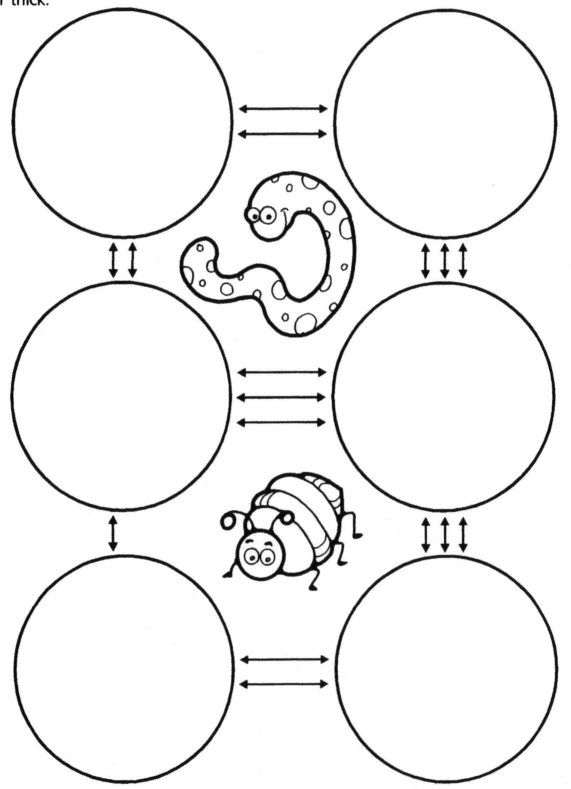

Name _____

I began this unit on sets on _____ .

Mark off each activity after you have completed it and after it has been checked. Hand in all pages when you finish the unit.

| Lesson | Completed | Checked |
|---|---|---|
| 1. Introduction to Sets | _____ | _____ |
| 2. Buggy | _____ | _____ |
| 3. Set Attributes | _____ | _____ |
| 4. Design a Set | _____ | _____ |
| 5. Introducing Subsets | _____ | _____ |
| 6. Writing Subsets | _____ | _____ |
| 7. Drawing Subsets | _____ | _____ |
| 8. Introducing Intersection Diagrams | _____ | _____ |
| 9. Words and Letters | _____ | _____ |
| 10. Divisible Sets | _____ | _____ |
| 11. Describing the Intersection | _____ | _____ |
| 12. Intersecting Imaginative Things | _____ | _____ |
| 13. Sets with Real Things | _____ | _____ |
| 14. More Real Sets | _____ | _____ |

I completed the unit on_____ .

Name _____

A **set** is a collection or group of people, numbers or things. The members of the set are like each other in at least one way.

Look at the numbers inside and outside the set. You will see that the numbers that belong to the set are **even numbers**.

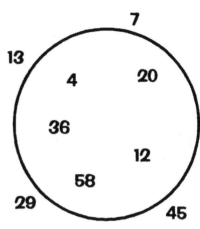

1. Write all the even numbers listed below inside the circle to show they belong in the set. Write the odd numbers outside the circle to show they do not belong in the set.

| | | |
|---|---|---|
| 14 | 56 | 129 |
| 27 | 61 | 112 |
| 39 | 22 | 70 |
| 44 | 19 | 75 |

**Even Numbers**

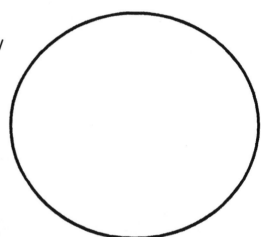

2. Write all the letters listed below inside or outside of the circle so the circle contains the set of vowels.

| | | |
|---|---|---|
| B | E | Q |
| F | Z | U |
| O | M | D |
| J | A | R |
| K | I | C |

**Vowels**

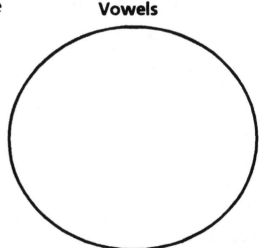

Name _____

Study the creatures in each set and decide why they belong together.

**1**

All the creatures in this set have

_____

**2**

All the creatures in this set have

_____

**3**

All the creatures in this set have

_____

**4**

All the creatures in this set have

_____

**5**

All the creatures in this set have

_____

**6**

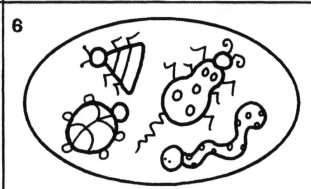

All the creatures in this set have

_____

Name _____

Sometimes there may be more than one attribute needed for set membership. Examine the sets below. Look at the things outside of the set as well as the members that belong to the set. Decide what two attributes are needed to belong to each set.

1. The members of Set A all have

_____

   and

_____

2. The members of Set B all have

_____

   and

_____

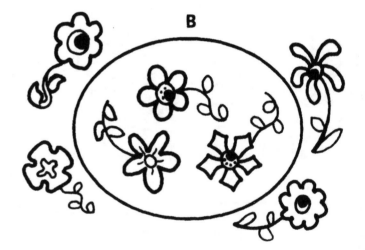

3. The members of Set C all have

_____

   and

_____

**Design a Set**

Name _____

Use the circles below to create your own sets. Draw things
outside the circle that do not belong to the set.

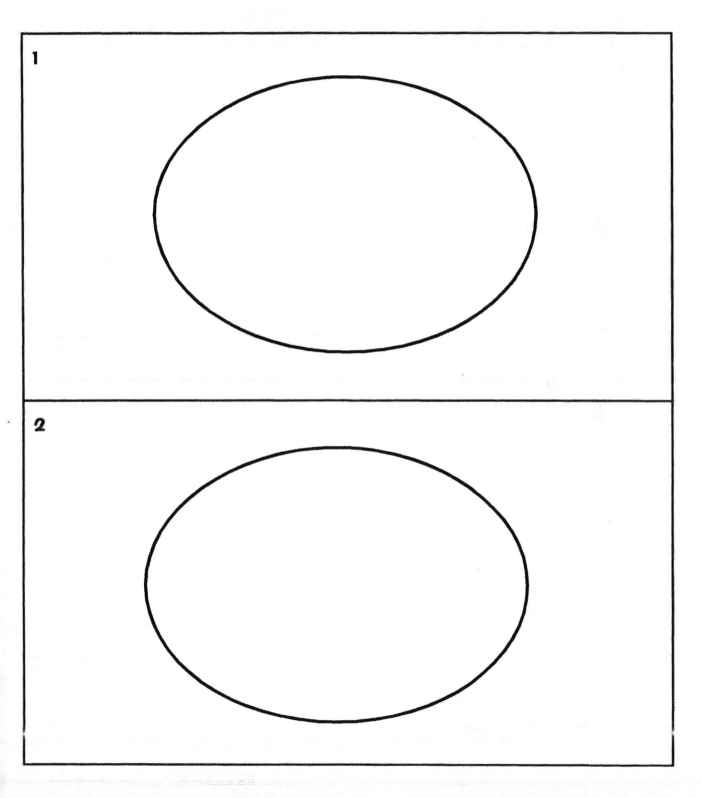

Name _____

Sometimes a set of things is a part of a larger set. We call the smaller set the **subset**.

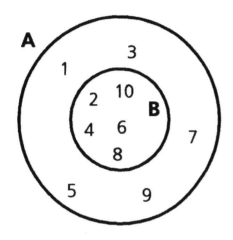

Set A is all the numbers between 1 and 10.
Set B is all the even numbers between 1 and 10
We say set B is a **subset** of set A.

Describe these sets.

1. Set C is the set of things that

_____

Set D is the set of things that

_____

Set _____ is a subset of set _____.

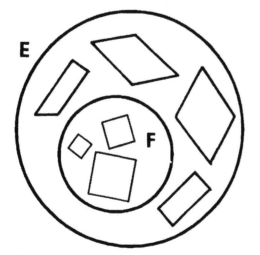

2. Set E is the set of things that

_____

Set F is the set of things that

_____

Set _____ is a subset of set _____.

Name _____

Write words, letters and numbers in the correct circle to show the sets and subsets.

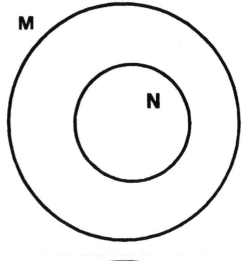

1. Set M = (a, b, c, d, e, f, g, h, i)

   Set N = (a, e, i)

   Set N is a _____ of set M.

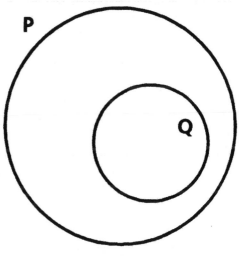

2. Set P = (5, 10, 15, 20, 25, 30, 35)

   Set Q = (10, 20, 30)

   Set Q is a subset of set _____.

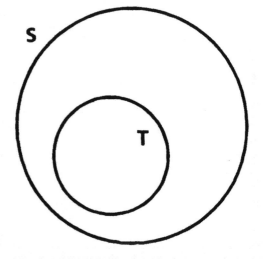

3. Set S = (boy, boat, box, balloon, bean)

   Set T = (boy, box)

   Set T is a _____ of set S.

Name _____

Draw or write at least two things in each of the circles to show the sets and subsets.

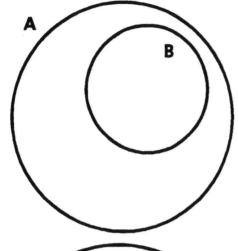

1. Set A = (numbers between 4 and 12)

   Set B = (even numbers between 4 and  12)

   Set _____ is a subset of set _____.

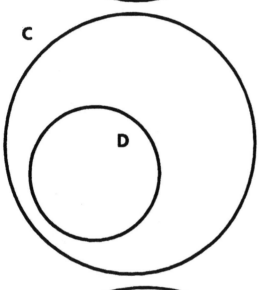

2. Set C = (circles with stripes)

   Set D = (circles with stripes and dots)

   Set_____ has more things in it than set _____.

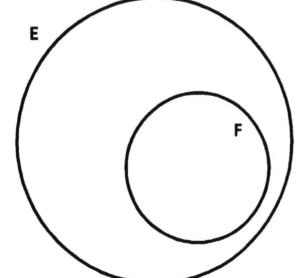

3. Set E = (names of five people in your class)

   Set F = (names of two girls in your class)

   Set E has _____ things in it.

   Set F has _____ things in it.

Name _____

The number 12 has the digit 2 and it is also an even number. It belongs to both sets.

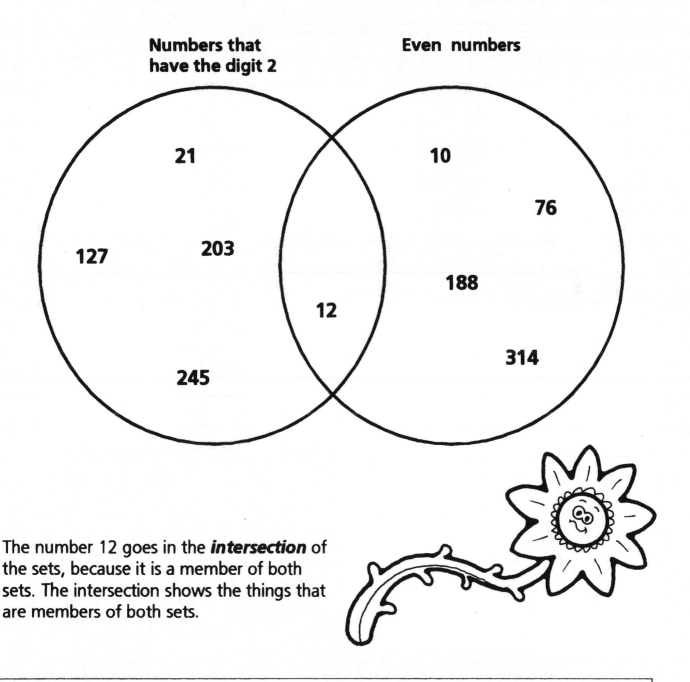

**Numbers that
have the digit 2**

**Even numbers**

21

10

76

127

203

188

12

314

245

The number 12 goes in the **intersection** of the sets, because it is a member of both sets. The intersection shows the things that are members of both sets.

Place these numbers where they belong in the Venn diagram above.

129     40     200     92     121     26     239     118     234

Name _____

1. Put the letters in the box
   where they belong in the
   sets.

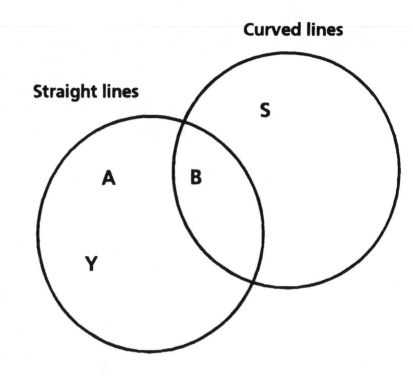

2. Write these words where they belong in the Venn diagram below.

| goat | cot | he | bread | night | hat |
|------|-----|-----|-------|-------|-----|
| knit | find | lake | wrote | gnat | met |

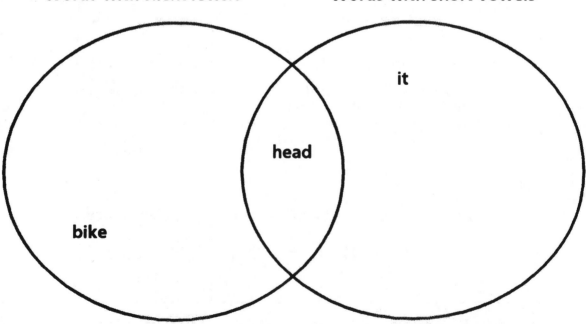

Name _____

1. The numbers in the box below can all be evenly divided by 2 or by 5. Some can be evenly divided by both 2 and 5. Put all the numbers where they belong in the diagram.

| 20 | 14 | 28 | 40 | 32 | 15 | 44 | 60 | 55 |
|----|----|----|----|----|----|----|----|----|
| 18 | 62 | 35 | 46 | 50 | 38 | 25 | 30 | 65 |

**Divisible by 2**                                    **Divisible by 5**

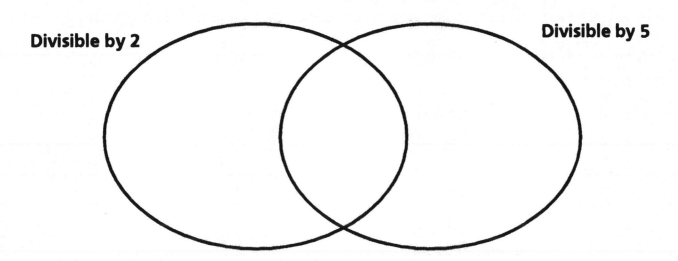

2. Place the numbers in the box below where they belong in the Venn diagram.

| 42 | 52 | 36 | 63 | 28 | 45 | 51 | 18 | 34 |
|----|----|----|----|----|----|----|----|----|
| 33 | 48 | 56 | 27 | 38 | 60 | 16 | 39 | 21 |

**Divisible by 2**                                    **Divisible by 3**

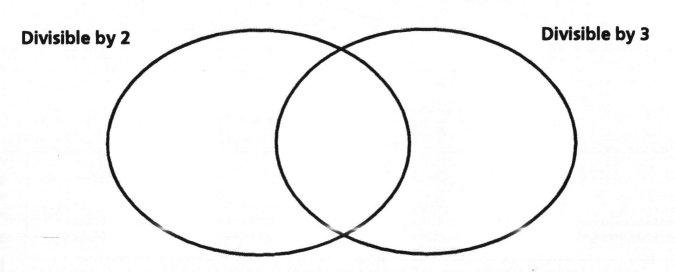

Name _____

Decide what is alike about all the members in each set. Then name each set.

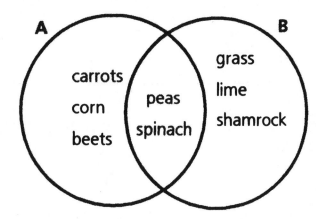

1. Set A is a set of _____.

Set B is a set of _____.

The intersection of set A and set B

is a set of _____

_____.

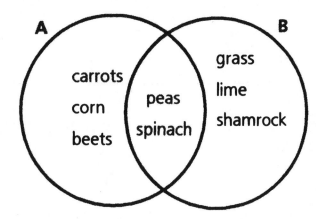

2. Set C is a set of _____.

Set D is a set of _____.

The intersection of set C and set D

is a set of _____

_____.

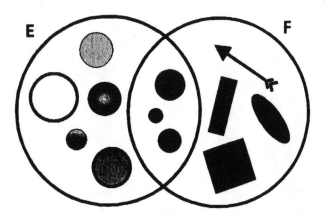

3. Set E is a set of _____.

Set F is a set of _____.

The intersection of set E and set F

is a set of _____

_____.

**Intersecting Imaginative Things**

Name _____

Analyze the sets in the diagrams below. Decide what attribute is necessary to belong to each set. Circle the figures on the left that would belong in the intersection of the sets.

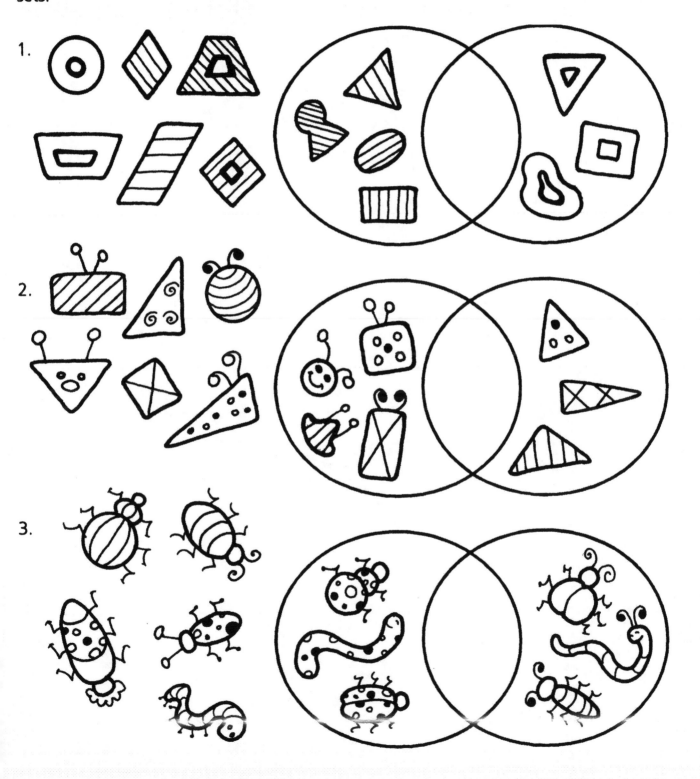

Name _____

Write several things that would be in each set. Think of at least two things that would be in both sets. Write them in the intersection of the two sets.

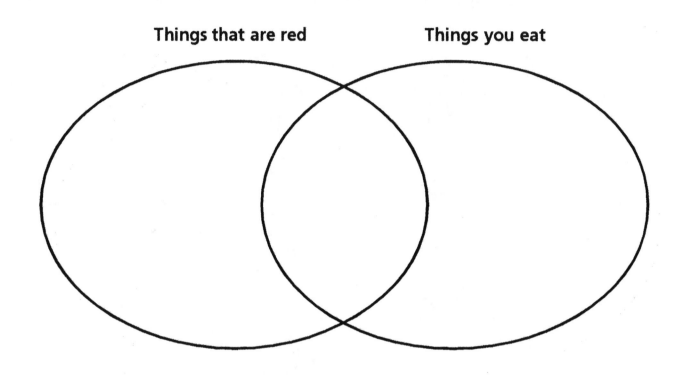

**Things that are red**        **Things you eat**

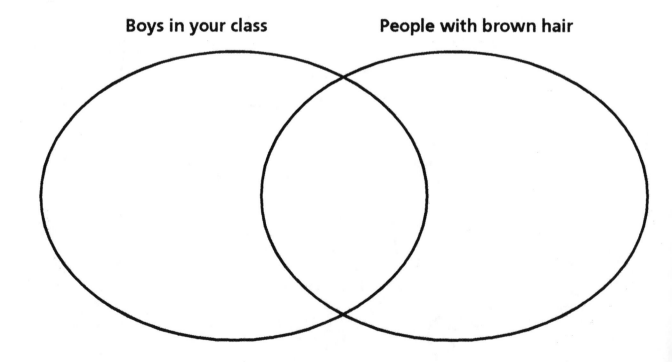

**Boys in your class**        **People with brown hair**

Name _____

Write several things that would be in each set. Think of at least two things that would be in both sets. Write them in the intersection of the two sets.

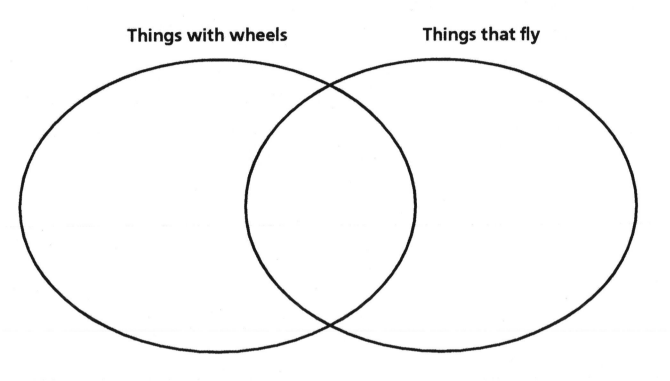

**Things with wheels**          **Things that fly**

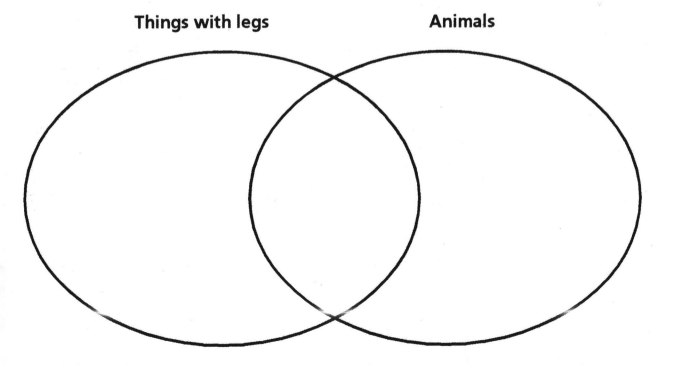

**Things with legs**          **Animals**

Name _____

I began this unit on tangrams on _____ .

When you have completed a tangram puzzle, have someone look at it to make sure the pieces fit. Then have that person write his or her initials on the chart below.

| *Puzzle* | *Checked by* | *Puzzle* | *Checked by* |
|---|---|---|---|
| Rectangles and Triangles | _____ | Soaring Bird | _____ |
| Squares | _____ | Fancy Fish | _____ |
| The Robot | _____ | Fish | _____ |
| Flower Pot | _____ | Barn | _____ |
| Roof | _____ | Ice Cream Cone | _____ |
| Dinosaur | _____ | | _____ |

**Special Project** - Use the seven tangram pieces to create an object. Trace around the shape. Use the shape to create a picture. Have a friend try to fit the puzzle pieces over the shape you created.

I completed this unit on _____

DOI: 10.4324/9781003235019-4

Name

A **tangram** is a Chinese puzzle consisting of a square cut into seven pieces – five triangles, a square, and a rhomboid. The pieces can be put together to form different figures.

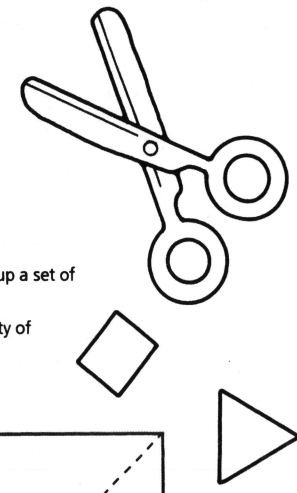

- Cut out the square below.

- Carefully cut on the dotted lines.

- You will have the seven pieces that make up a set of tangrams.

- These shapes can be arranged into a variety of figures and designs.

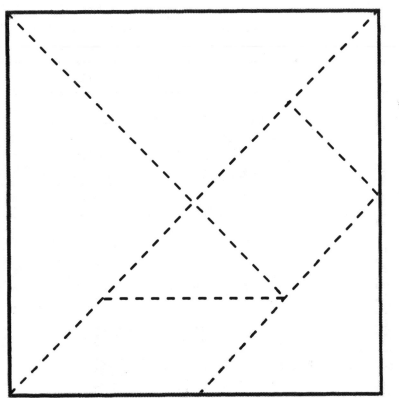

Name _____

Use **three tangram pieces** to make each shape in a different way. Trace around the shapes to show what pieces you used.

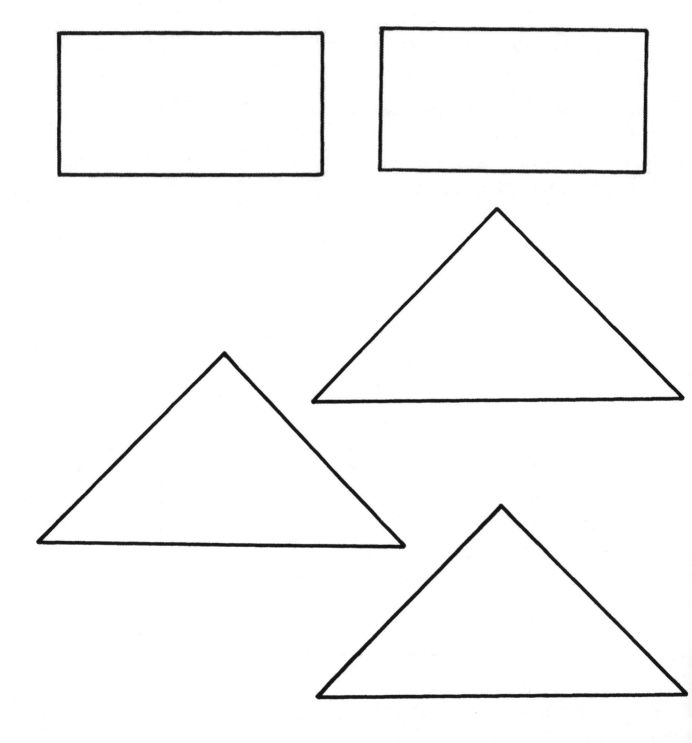

Name _____

Make the squares below three different ways. Trace around the shapes to show the pieces you used.

Use two pieces

Use five pieces

Use four pieces

Name _____

Use the seven tangram pieces to make the shape below.

Name _____

Use the seven tangram pieces to make the shape below.

Name _____

Use the seven tangram pieces to make the shape below.

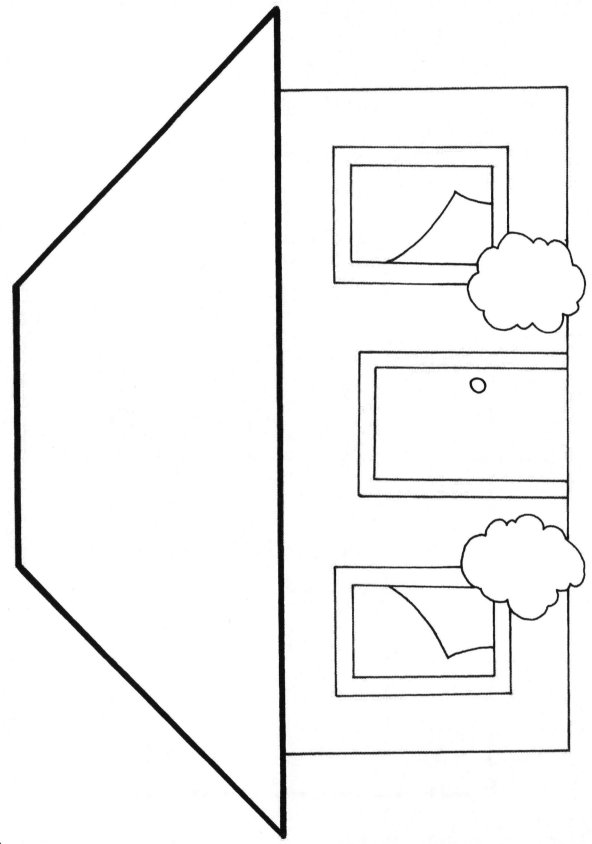

Name _____

Use the seven tangram pieces to make the shape below.

Name _____

Use the seven tangram pieces to make the shape below.

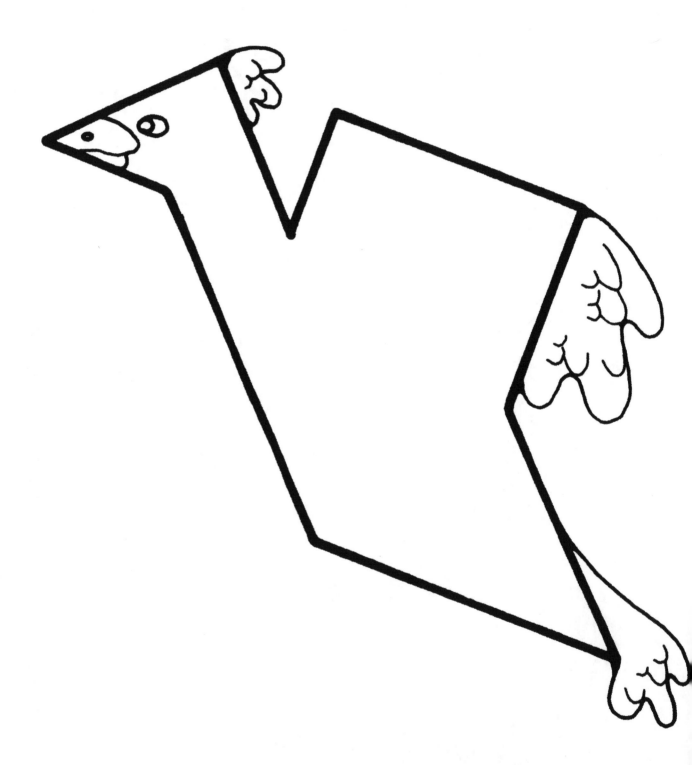

Name _____

Use the seven tangram pieces to make the shape below.

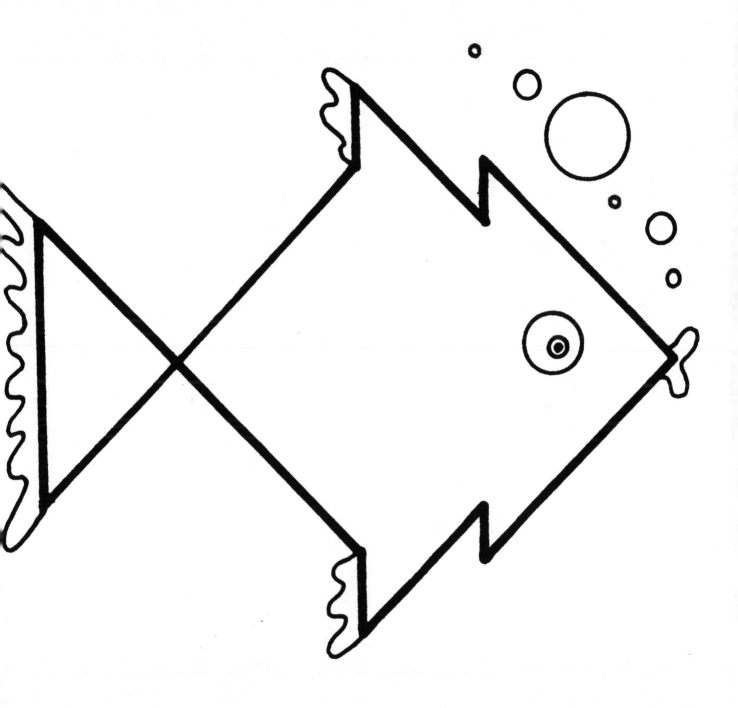

Use the seven
tangram pieces to
make the shape to
the left.

Name _____

Use the seven tangram pieces to make the shape below.

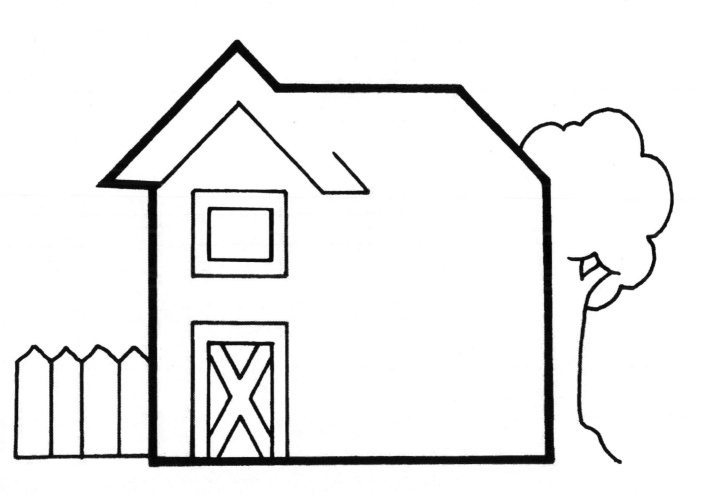

Name _____

Use the seven tangram
pieces to make the
shape to the right.

Name _____

I began this unit on Egyptian numbers on _____ .

Mark off each activity after you have completed it and after it has been checked. Hand in all pages when you finish the unit.

| Lessons | Completed | Checked |
|---|---|---|
| 1. Introduction to Ancient Egypt | _____ | _____ |
| 2. Egyptian Numerals for 1, 10, 100 and 1,000 | _____ | _____ |
| 3. Matching Numbers | _____ | _____ |
| 4. The Pyramids | _____ | _____ |
| 5. News Headlines | _____ | _____ |
| 6. Writing Egyptian Numbers | _____ | _____ |
| 7. Larger Egyptian Numbers | _____ | _____ |
| 8. Using 10,000 and 100,000 | _____ | _____ |
| 9. Adding Numbers | _____ | _____ |
| 10. Matching Numbers | _____ | _____ |
| 11. The Sphinx | _____ | _____ |
| 12. Make Your Own | _____ | _____ |

I completed this unit on _____

Name _____

In ancient Egypt the people lived along the banks of the Nile River. They developed large farms, prosperous markets, big cities, and a system of government. They needed a system of writing to keep records for trading and government.

They developed a system of writing called **hieroglyphics** that used picture symbols, or hieroglyphs, to represent the numbers one, ten, and powers of ten. Some of those symbols were:

| 1 | I | (a staff) |
| 10 | ∩ | (an arch) |
| 100 | ૭ | (a coiled rope) |
| 1,000 | ⚘ | (a flower) |

The ancient Egyptians' number system differed from ours in two main ways:

- They had no symbol for zero.

- They had no place value. Therefore, the symbols could be written in any order.

1,243 could be written ⚘૭૭∩∩∩∩III or III∩∩૭⚘૭∩∩∩

Match the Egyptian numbers below with the number written in our number system.

_____ 1.  ∩∩∩IIIIII                          a. 160

_____ 2.  ૭∩∩∩∩∩∩                          b. 74

_____ 3.  ∩∩∩∩∩∩∩IIII                    c. 4,220

_____ 4.  ૭૭૭∩∩∩∩∩IIII                  d. 2,112

_____ 5.  ⚘⚘⚘⚘૭૭∩∩                        e. 35

_____ 6.  ⚘⚘૭∩II                              f. 434

**Egyptian Numerals for 1, 10, 100 and 1,000**

Name _____

| 1 | I | (staff) |
| 10 | ∩ | (arch) |
| 100 | ℂ | (rope) |
| 1,000 | ⚘ | (flower) |

Study the Egyptian numbers below and write what they equal in our number system.

1. ℂ∩∩∩∩∩III  _____

2. ℂℂℂℂℂ∩∩IIIII  _____

3. ⚘ℂℂ∩∩∩IIII  _____

4. ⚘ℂℂℂ∩∩∩∩∩∩  _____

5. IIIIII∩∩∩∩∩∩∩ℂ⚘⚘  _____

6. ∩∩∩∩∩∩∩ℂℂ⚘⚘⚘⚘  _____

7. IIIIIIIII∩∩∩∩∩⚘⚘⚘  _____

8. ⚘⚘ℂℂℂℂℂℂ∩IIIII  _____

9. IIIIIIIIII∩∩⚘  _____

10. ∩∩∩∩∩∩∩ℂℂℂ⚘⚘⚘⚘⚘  _____

11. ⚘⚘⚘⚘⚘⚘ℂℂ∩∩∩IIIII  _____

12. ⚘⚘⚘⚘⚘⚘⚘⚘⚘⚘∩∩∩∩∩  _____

Name _____

Use this chart of Egyptian numerals to help you match numbers written in our number system with those written in the ancient Egyptian system. Write the correct letter on the blank on the left.

| 1 | I |
|---|---|
| 10 | ∩ |
| 100 | ϩ |
| 1,000 | ⚶ |

_____ 1.  ⚶⚶⚶ϩϩ ϩϩϩϩ

_____ 2.  ϩϩ∩∩∩∩∩∩∩ϩϩII

_____ 3.  ∩∩∩∩∩∩

_____ 4.  ⚶⚶⚶ϩϩϩϩϩϩ∩∩∩I

_____ 5.  ∩∩∩∩III

_____ 6.  ⚶⚶II

_____ 7.  ⚶⚶⚶⚶∩∩∩∩∩∩

_____ 8.  ϩ∩∩∩∩III

_____ 9.  ⚶⚶⚶∩∩∩∩

_____ 10.  IIIIIIII

_____ 11.  ϩϩϩϩϩϩ∩∩∩

_____ 12.  ∩∩∩∩∩∩∩I

A. 8

B. 43

C. 71

D. 143

E. 272

F. 60

G. 640

H. 2,002

I. 2,531

J. 4,060

K. 4,600

L. 3,040

Name _____

Read the information about the ancient Egyptian pyramids. Whenever you come to an Egyptian number, write the number it would equal in our number system.

The kings in ancient Egypt were called

pharaohs. When a pharaoh died, he was buried

in a huge tomb called a pyramid. The first of

these monumental royal tombs was the Step Pyramid of King Zoser. It was built

about ⚡⚡ʕʕʕʕʕʕʕ∩∩IIIII (_____) B.C. These early pyramids

were built of successive layers of stone, like enormous steps.

Later Egyptian pyramids had IIII (_____) triangular sides that met

at a point at the top. The Pyramid of Pharaoh Kahfre was built about

⚡⚡ʕʕʕʕʕ∩∩∩ (_____) B.C. It is ʕ∩∩∩IIIIIII (_____) meters

or ʕʕʕʕ∩∩∩∩IIIIIII (_____) feet high.

The largest tomb is the Great Pyramid of Pharaoh Khufu. It is one of the IIIIIII

(_____) Wonders of the Ancient World. It is ʕ∩∩∩∩IIIIIIII

(_____) meters or ʕʕʕʕ∩∩∩∩∩∩∩I (_____) feet high.

The square base measures ʕʕ∩∩∩ (_____) meters or

ʕʕʕʕʕʕ∩∩∩∩∩IIIIII (_____) feet on each side.

Egyptian pyramids were built without the aid of cranes or any modern equipment

from about ⚡⚡ʕʕʕʕʕʕ (_____) B.C. to about ⚡ (_____) B.C. The

remains of ∩∩∩∩∩∩∩ (_____) of these ⚡⚡⚡ (_____)

to ⚡⚡⚡⚡⚡ (_____) year-old pyramids still remain in Egypt and Sudan.

Name _____

Here are some headlines from the Egyptian Tribune. Write the Egyptian numbers for these newspaper headlines.

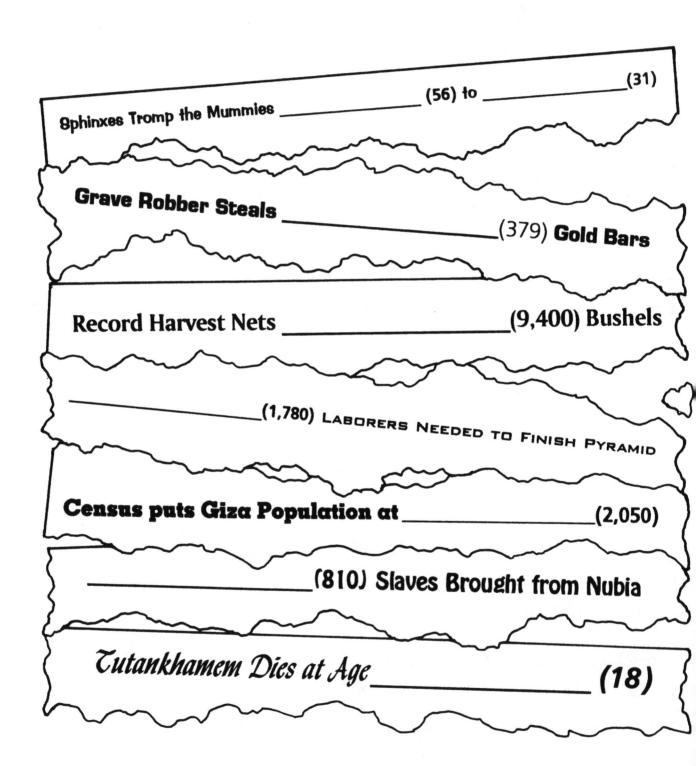

Sphinxes Tromp the Mummies _____ (56) to _____ (31)

Grave Robber Steals _____ (379) Gold Bars

Record Harvest Nets _____ (9,400) Bushels

_____ (1,780) Laborers Needed to Finish Pyramid

Census puts Giza Population at _____ (2,050)

_____ (810) Slaves Brought from Nubia

Tutankhamem Dies at Age _____ (18)

**Writing Egyptian Numerals**

Name _____

_____
_____

| | |
|---|---|
| 1= | \| |
| 10= | ∩ |
| 100= | ℓ |
| 1000= | ⸙ |

Write the Egyptian numeral for the following things. Also write the answers in our number system.

1. Your age _____ _____

2. Today's date (month/day/year)_____ _____

3. The number of students in your class _____ _____

4. The number of days in a year _____ _____

5. The year your school was built _____ _____

6. The cost of a pack of gum_____ _____

7. The year you started school_____ _____

8. The number of chairs in your school room _____ _____

9. The number of students in your school _____ _____

10. The number of pages in your math book _____ _____

11. The cost of a pair of jeans _____ _____

Name _____

The Egyptians needed only one symbol for 10,000 and one symbol for 100,000. The symbols looked like this:

(     (a bent finger) = 10,000

⌒     (a tadpole) = 100,000

So  543,210 was written  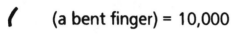

And 123,456 was written  

Write the Egyptian numerals below in our number system.

1. ( (         _____

2. ⌒ ( (       _____

3. ( ( ( ( ( ¥ ¥ ¥ ς ς ς ∩ ∩ ∩     _____

4. ( ( ( ( ( ¥ ¥ ¥ ς ∩ ∩ ∩ | | | | |     _____

5. ⌒ ⌒ ( ( ( ¥ ς ς ∩ ∩ ∩ ∩ ∩     _____

6. ⌒ ⌒ ⌒ ( ( ¥ ¥ ¥ ¥ ¥ ∩ ∩     _____

7. ( ( ( ( ( ( ( ¥ ¥ ¥ ς ς ς ς ς ∩ | | | | |     _____

8. | | | ∩ ∩ ∩ ∩ ς ς ς ¥ ( ( ⌒     _____

9. | | ∩ ∩ ∩ ∩ ∩ ∩ ς ¥ ¥ ¥ ( ( ( ( (     _____

10. ∩ ∩ ¥ ¥ ⌒ ⌒     _____

**56**

Name _____

Use **<** (less than), **>** (greater than) or **=** to compare the numbers below.

1. ⦚⦚⦚ ⦚⦚⦚ ∩∩ ◯ ⦚⦚ ⦚⦚⦚⦚⦚⦚ ⦚⦚ ∩∩∩∩

2. ⌒ ⦚⦚ ⦚⦚⦚ ◯ ⌒ ⦚⦚⦚ ⦚⦚

3. ∩∩⦚⦚⦚⦚⦚ ⦚⦚⦚⦚ ◯ ⦚⦚⦚⦚ ⦚⦚⦚∩∩

4. ⌒⌒⌒ ◯ ∩∩∩∩∩⦚⦚⦚ ⦚⦚⦚⦚⦚ ⦚⦚⦚⦚ ⌒

5. ⌒ ⦚⦚⦚⦚⦚⦚⦚⦚⦚⦚ ◯ ⌒ ⦚

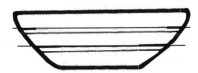

Write these numbers in the Egyptian number system.

6. 60,050 _____

7. 15,000 _____

8. 300,000 _____

9. 150,000 _____

10. 245,300 _____

11. 303,030 _____

Name _____

Using the Egyptian number system, write the number that

1. comes after 9,999 _____

2. comes after 29,999 _____

3. comes after 999 _____


Using the Egyptian number system, write the number that is

4. 100 more than 20,000 _____

5. 1,000 more than 34,000 _____

6. 10,000 more than 100,000 _____

7. 1,000 more than 250,000 _____

8. 5,000 more than 5,000 _____

9. 50,000 more than 50,000 _____

10. 1,000 more than 235,000 _____

11. 300 more than 3,003_____

**Matching Numbers**

Name _____

Each Egyptian number on the left equals one of the numbers in our number system on the right. Match the two numbers and write the correct letter on the line.

_____ 1.      A. 11

_____ 2.      B. 101

_____ 3.      C. 1,010

_____ 4      D. 10,100

_____ 5.      E. 11,010

_____ 6.      F. 100,100

_____ 7.      G. 110,001

_____ 8.      H. 212

_____ 9.      I. 2,020

_____ 10.      J. 20,200

_____ 11.      K. 22,020

_____ 12.      L. 200,222

_____ 13.      M. 202,002

_____ 14.      N. 220,200

Name _____

Fill in the missing letters using the code written in Egyptian numbers.

### Code

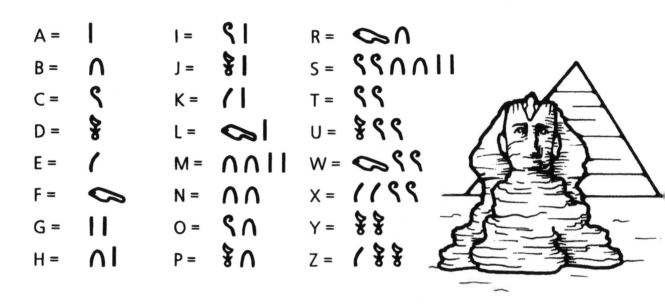

| | | |
|---|---|---|
| A = | I = | R = |
| B = | J = | S = |
| C = | K = | T = |
| D = | L = | U = |
| E = | M = | W = |
| F = | N = | X = |
| G = | O = | Y = |
| H = | P = | Z = |

Sphinxes were _____ _____ _____ _____ _____ _____ _____
          222     200     1     200    1,200  10,000    222

with the _____ _____ _____ of a _____ _____ _____ _____ and
    10    110   1000   2000    100,001  101   110   20

_____ _____ _____ _____ of a _____ _____ _____. They represented
  11   10,000   1   1,000    22   1   20

_____ _____ _____ _____. The _____ _____ _____ _____ _____
  2   110   1000  222    2  100,010  10,000  1  200

_____ _____ _____ _____ _____ _____ of _____ _____ _____ _____
 222  1010  11  101  20  20,200    2   101  12,000  1

is the most famous.

It is _____ _____ _____ _____ _____ – _____ _____ _____ feet high
  222   101  20,200  200  2000    222   101  20,200

and _____ _____ _____ hundred _____ _____ _____ _____ _____
  200  100,200  110     100,000  110  100,010  200  2000

feet long.

Name _____

Use this space to write one of the following things. Use as many numbers as you can and write the numbers in the ancient Egyptian number system. Give your finished product to a friend and ask the friend to decode what you have written. Decorate the bottom of your paper with an ancient Egyptian design.

- An advertisement

- A want ad for something you want to sell

- A want ad that might appear in an ancient Egyptian newspaper

- A note to a friend

| | |
|---|---|
| 1 = | I |
| 10 = | ∩ |
| 100 = | ? |
| 1,000 = | ? |
| 10,000 = | ( |
| 100,000 = | ? |

# Answers

## Attribute Blocks
### Lesson 1-2- pages 6 - 7
Check to see that block is drawn according to directions.
### Lesson 3 - page 8

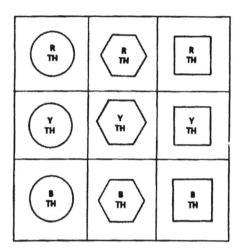

### Lesson 4 - page 9

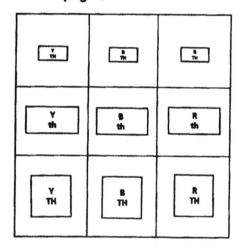

### Lessons 5-15 - pages 10 - 20
Answers will vary. Check to see that blocks differ from the adjacent blocks according to the directions.

## Sets and Venn Diagrams
### Lesson 1 - page 22
1. inside - 14, 22, 44, 56, 70, 112
   outside - 19, 27, 39, 61, 75, 129
2. inside - A, E, I, O, U
   outside - B, C, D, F, J, K, M, Q, R, Z

### Lesson 2 - page 23
1. spots      2. tails
3. stripes      4. six legs
5. triangles      6. round heads

### Lesson 3 - page 24
1 center design, 2 stripes.
2. 5 petals, 3 leaves
3. smiles, hair

### Lesson 4 - page 25
Answers will vary depending on which items students chose to draw in their sets. All members of the set should have a common characteristic and items outside of the set should not have this characteristic.

### Lesson 5 - page 26
1. C - triangles; D - triangles with equal sides; Set D is a subset of set C.
2. E - things with 4 sides (quadrilaterals); F -squares; Set is a subset of set E.

### Lesson 6 - page 27
Check to see that elements of the subset have been placed in the smaller circle and all remaining elements are in the larger circle.
1. subset      2. P
3. Set S is a set of words that begin with the letter b; Set T is three letter words that begin with B; subset

### Lesson 7 - page 28
Check to see that elements of the subset have been placed in the smaller circle and all remaining elements are in the larger circle.
1. Set B is a subset of set A.
2. Set C has more things that set D.
3. E - 5; F - 2

### Lesson 8 - page 29
With 2 digit - 129, 121, 239,
Intersection - 200, 92, 26, 234
Even - 40, 118

### Lesson 9 - page 30
1. Straight lines - N, I, K, F, E, V, T, M, H, L
   intersection - D, G, P, R, Q, J
   curved lines - O, C,
2. silent letters - lake, goat, wrote, night
   intersection - knit, bread, gnat
   short vowels - cot, hat, met
   outside both sets - he, find

### Lesson 10 - page 31
1. divisible by 2 - 14, 28, 32, 44, 18, 62, 46, 38,
   intersection - 20, 40, 60, 50, 30
   divisible by 5 - 15, 55, 35, 25, 65
2. divisible by 2 - 52, 28, 34, 56, 38, 16,
   intersection - 42, 36, 18, 48, 60,
   divisible by 3 - 63, 45, 51, 33, 27, 39, 21

### Lesson 11 - page 32
1. A - vegetables; B - green things; intersection - green vegetables
2. C - things that fly; D - animals; intersection - animals that fly (birds)
3. E - circles; F - black things; intersection -black circles

### Lesson 12 - page 33
1. necessary attributes - lines and same shape in the center
2. necessary attributes - triangular body and antenna
3. necessary attributes - dots and antenna

**Lesson 13 - 14 - page 34 - 35**
answers will vary

## Tangram Puzzles

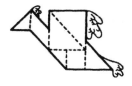

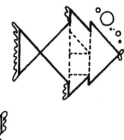

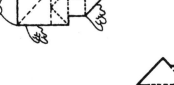

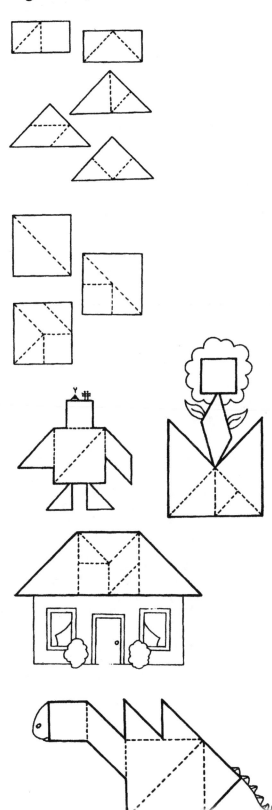

## Ancient Egyptian Numbers

**Lesson 1 - page 50**

| | |
|---|---|
| 1. e | 4. f |
| 2. a | 5. c |
| 3. b | 6. d |

**Lesson 2 - page 51**

| | |
|---|---|
| 1. 163 | 7. 3,056 |
| 2. 525 | 8. 2,515 |
| 3. 1,234 | 9. 1,029 |
| 4. 1,350 | 10. 5,360 |
| 5. 2,163 | 11. 6,235 |
| 6. 4,170 | 12. 9,060 |

## Lesson 3 - page 52

| | |
|---|---|
| 1. K | 7. J |
| 2. E | 8. D |
| 3. F | 9. L |
| 4. I | 10. A |
| 5. B | 11. G |
| 6. H | 12. C |

## Lesson 4 - page 53

2,725 B. C.
4 triangular steps
2,530 B. C.
136 meters or 446 feet
7 wonders
147 meters or 481 feet
230 meters or 756 feet
2,700 B. C. to 1,000 B. C.
70
3,000 to 5,000 year old

## Lesson 5 - page 54

1. ∩∩∩∩∩IIIIII ; ∩∩∩I
2. ϨϨϨ ∩∩∩∩∩∩∩ IIIIIIIII
3. ϨϨϨϨϨϨϨϨ ϤϤϤϤ
4. Ϩ ϤϤϤϤϤϤϤϤ ∩∩∩∩∩∩∩
5. ϨϨ ∩∩∩∩∩
6. ϤϤϤϤϤϤϤϤ∩
7. ∩IIIIIIII

## Lesson 6 - page 55

Answers will vary.

## Lesson 7 - page 56

| | |
|---|---|
| 1. 20,000 | 6. 325,020 |
| 2. 120,000 | 7. 72,515 |
| 3. 42,340 | 8. 121,343 |
| 4. 53,135 | 9. 53,162 |
| 5. 231,250 | 10. 202,020 |

## Lesson 8 - page 57

| | |
|---|---|
| 1. > | 4. > |
| 2. < | 5. < |
| 3. = | |

6. IIIIII∩∩∩∩
7. IϨϨϨϨϨ
8. ⌇⌇⌇
9. ⌇IIIII
10. ⌇⌇IIIIϨϨϨϨϨϤϤϤ
11. ⌇⌇⌇ϨϨϨ∩∩

## Lesson 9 - page 58

1. I
2. III
3. Ϩ
4. IIϤ
5. IIIϨϨϨϨϨ
6. ⌇I
7. ⌇⌇IIIIII
8. I
9. ⌇
10. ⌇⌇III ϨϨϨϨϨ
11. ϨϨϨ ϤϤϤ III

## Lesson 10 - page 59

| | |
|---|---|
| 1. C | 8. J |
| 2. E | 9. L |
| 3. G | 10. I |
| 4. A | 11. H |
| 5. B | 12. K |
| 6. F | 13. N |
| 7. D | 14. M |

## Lesson 11 - page 60

| | | |
|---|---|---|
| A = 1 | B = 10 | C = 10 |
| D = 1,000 | E = 10,000 | F = 100,000 |
| G = 2 | H = 11 | I = 101 |
| J = 1,001 | K = 10,001 | L = 100,001 |
| M = 22 | N = 20 | O = 110 |
| P = 1,010 | R = 100,010 | S = 222 |
| T = 200 | U = 1,200 | W = 100,200 |
| X = 20,200 | Y = 2,000 | Z = 12,000 |

Sphinxes were **statues** with the **body** of a **lion** and **head** of a **man**. They represented **gods**. The **Great sphinx** of **Giza** is the most famous.
It is **sixty-six** feet high and **two** hundred **forty** feet long.

## Lesson 12 - page 61

Answers will vary

Printed in the United States
by Baker & Taylor Publisher Services